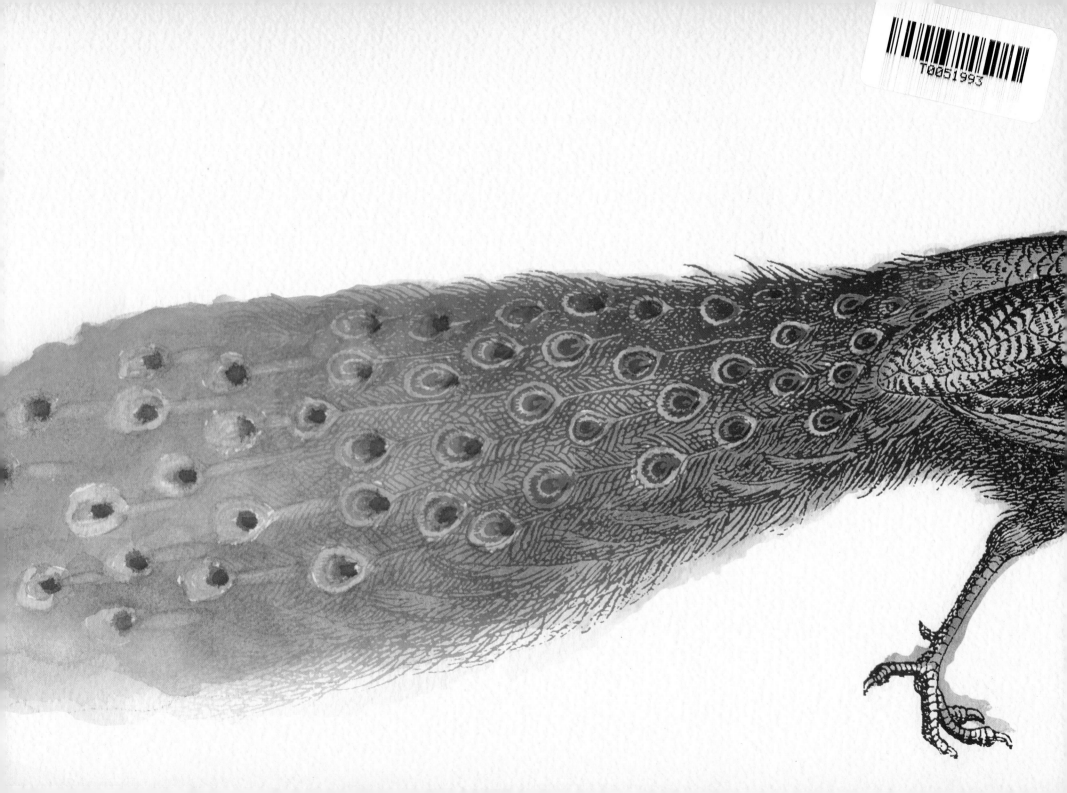

For
Ann + Raphael

First U.S. edition 2018
First published by Berbay Publishing (Australia) 2017

Library of Congress Catalog Card Number pending
ISBN 978-1-5362-0033-1

18 19 20 21 22 23 TLF 10 9 8 7 6 5 4 3 2 1

Printed in Dongguan, Guangdong, China

This book was typeset in Passport.
The illustrations were done in watercolor and were
adapted from nineteenth-century artwork. The original
illustrations were sourced from Getty Images (peacock) and
*Animals: 1,419 Copyright-Free Illustrations of Mammals,
Birds, Fish, Insects, Etc.* (New York: Dover, 1979).

Candlewick Press
99 Dover Street
Somerville, Massachusetts 02144

visit us at www.candlewick.com

HEADS
and
TAILS

John Canty

CANDLEWICK PRESS

I have long furry ears
and a small nose.

I live in a burrow
in the ground.

I have a white
fluffy tail.

I AM A...

RABBIT.

I am covered with
slippery scales.

I am long and thin.

My bite can
be poisonous.

I AM A ...

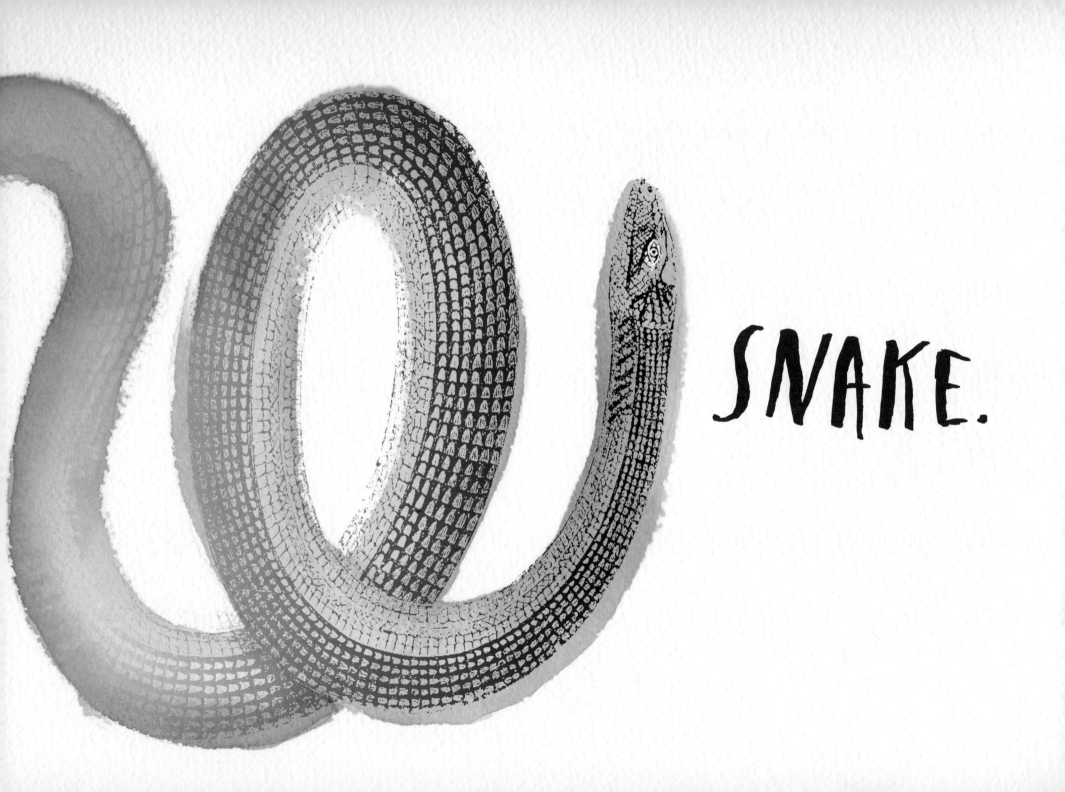

SNAKE.

I have a striped
furry coat.

I live in
the jungle.

I am the largest
of all cats.

I AM A...

TIGER.

I live in water.

I breathe with
my gills.

I swim with
my fins.

I AM A . . .

FISH.

I have a big horn
on my nose.

I have a thick,
rough hide.

I roll in mud
to stay cool.

I AM A . . .

RHINOCEROS.

I am enormous.

I am heavy.

I have big ears
and a long trunk.

I AM A...

AN...

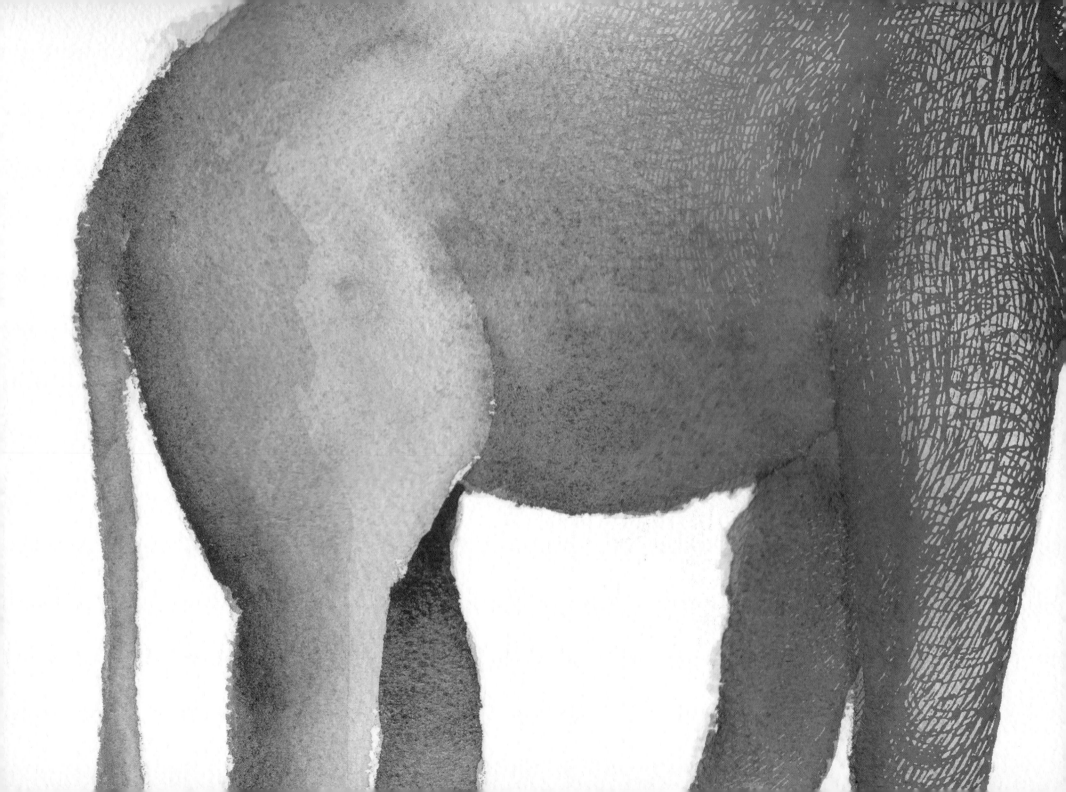

ELEPHANT.

I have a hard shell.

I live on land.

I move slowly.

I AM A . . .

TORTOISE.

I love chasing mice.

I have soft fur
and a long tail.

I purr.

I AM A . . .

CAT.

I have a strong scaly tail.

I have powerful jaws
and small legs.

I have rows of
sharp teeth.

I AM A...

CROCODILE.

I am tall.

I have spots all over me.

I have long, thin legs.

I AM . . .

A...

GIRAFFE.

I have a big bushy tail.

I have a beautiful furry coat.

I am clever.

I AM A . . .

FOX.

I can hop
and swim.

I can croak loudly.

I have large eyes
to see all around me.

I AM A ...

FROG.

I have a pouch that I keep my baby in.

I have a long, strong tail.

I can hop very fast and very high.

I AM A...

KANGAROO.

I love to play.

I learn new things
every day.

I am growing.

I AM...